T0147156

Navigating the
NARROW WAY

CURTIS WILSON

WestBow
PRESS®
A DIVISION OF THOMAS NELSON
& ZONDERVAN

WestBow Press books may be ordered through booksellers or by contacting:

WestBow Press
A Division of Thomas Nelson & Zondervan
1663 Liberty Drive
Bloomington, IN 47403
www.westbowpress.com
844-714-3454

Because of the dynamic nature of the Internet, any web addresses or
links contained in this book may have changed since publication and
may no longer be valid. The views expressed in this work are solely those
of the author and do not necessarily reflect the views of the publisher,
and the publisher hereby disclaims any responsibility for them.

Any people depicted in stock imagery provided by Getty Images are
models, and such images are being used for illustrative purposes only.
Certain stock imagery © Getty Images.

Scripture quotations are from the ESV® Bible (The Holy Bible, English
Standard Version®), copyright © 2001 by Crossway, a publishing ministry
of Good News Publishers. Used by permission. All rights reserved.

ISBN: 978-1-6642-7932-2 (sc)
ISBN: 978-1-6642-7934-6 (hc)
ISBN: 978-1-6642-7933-9 (e)

Library of Congress Control Number: 2022917866

Print information available on the last page.

WestBow Press rev. date: 10/06/2022

Contents

Dedicated to my loving and faithful wife, Tabitha.

Who endured my personal transformation
process and treated every stage with grace.

He who finds a wife finds a good thing and obtains
favor from the Lord.

—Proverbs 18:22

Introduction

Centuries ago, someone created the word "disciple." This is a widely used title in Christianity. It means a learner or follower of Christ, someone who understands the teachings and can follow-through with life applications. In these lessons, we explore how God transforms us from everyday humans to extraordinary devotees. This transformation carries with it the ability to overcome the present world we live in and the enemy of our souls that we fight each day. It also allows us to exhibit a joy that can only come through a transformational process. Just as a meager caterpillar is changed to a beautiful butterfly, so the Lord wants to change the nature of who we are in our core beings. This is the context of 2 Corinthians 5, which says we are new creations in Christ.

To be discipled is to do away with the old life of sin and usher in the new way of life in Christ. Just as every country has laws and governance, so does the kingdom of God. As we come to know a new life in the kingdom, we also explore the beauty of participation within that domain.

The teachings shared in this book have been developed over several years and usually with a live audience involved in the process. As I have come to discover, there is one common denominator in the lives of those who have been devoted to God for a long period and seemed to have matured in their faith. That one commonality is that at a place in their Christian beginning, there was someone who walked with them and taught them the process of becoming a disciple of Jesus. This common theme is certainly scriptural, but sadly, it has become a dying skill set among the body of Christ. If you are a new believer, hopefully we can help you mature in your faith. If you are someone who has known the Lord for some time, then you can pick up new approaches to help you disciple someone else.

This book covers three basic transformations that occur with us, through us, and in us. They are transformation through relationship, transformation through community, and transformation through serving others. Each of these areas of our lives carry a unique and lasting effect on us. As you develop a personal relationship with Christ, you will be transformed into who you are under it all. As you grow to be part of the Christian community, you will learn how we are to influence each other. And finally, as you learn to serve, it will become evident what meaningful work is all about. This book is written in the form of a daily or weekly journal. I have added questions for you to meditate on and answer honestly. Be introspective in answering these questions, and you can learn along the way.

So fasten up, and prepare for the challenges of discipleship and living the life Christ purchased for you on the cross of Calvary.

Section 1

TRANSFORMATION THROUGH RELATIONSHIP

1

BORN INTO SIN

In the space below, write some of the details surrounding your conversion experience.

Was there a period leading up to your conversion when God put people or circumstances in your path to draw you to him?

For most of us who follow Jesus, there is a point in time that we can look back on and refer to as our salvation experiences. Thousands of narratives can be used to tell how we personally came to know him. Although each of our accounts of salvation are different, there is one thing that stays the same: Each of us has been transformed by the power of the gospel message. This personal transformation occurs in what seems like an instant. But if truth be told, it was a progression of God leading us to that moment. As we walk with the Lord and study his Word, we realize just how meticulous he is in bringing people to a knowledge of himself. I don't know if it is because he is not captured by time or if he is that confident in his own authority. Whatever the reason, God leads you and I down the path and sets us up to have an encounter with him. In this first lesson, I break down how we come to that redeeming knowledge. It will help you in recognizing when God is dealing with someone.

The first thing we must come to understand is that all humanity is born into sin. And that is a problem.

> Therefore, just as sin came into the world through one man, and death through sin, and so death spread to all men because all sinned. (Romans 5:12 ESV)

> For all have sinned and fall short of the glory of God. (Romans 3:23 ESV)

Because of this condition of our hearts, a separation occurred between us and our Creator long before we were born. Just as you did not pick your skin, eye, or hair colors, you did not get the choice of being born into sin. When we fail to recognize this truth, it suppresses all other truths the Lord is trying to reveal. This hardness of our hearts is the core of what God wants to change and transform. When someone tells us that they do not believe there is a God and argues the ridiculous notion that creation just happened, I point to what the scripture tells us regarding this ideology:

> For his invisible attributes, namely, his eternal power and divine nature, have been clearly perceived, ever since the creation of the world, in the things that have been made. So they are without excuse. (Romans 1:20 ESV)

Each person is without excuse because God has put a knowledge of himself into our hearts and embedded it into creation itself. The danger of present society is that we condone and justify our sins instead of acknowledging their grip on our lives.

Have you acknowledged and taken personal responsibility for the sin nature in your life?

Now that we can see the big picture, let's talk about the destructive nature of sin and how sin is defined in the Bible.

> For the wages of sin is death, but the free gift of God is eternal life in Christ Jesus our Lord. (Romans 6:23 ESV)

Perhaps we do not die an immediate death when we commit sin, but it certainly extracts the God-given life from us. Whether physical, emotional, or spiritual, this practice of lawlessness will slowly draw us into demise one decision at a time. Someone once said that "Sin will take you further than you wanted to go and keep you longer than you wanted to stay." Personally, I have found this to be true. Sin separates us from the only life-giving person—God the Father, Son, and Spirit. This separation causes destruction on every level because you are forced to make decisions, plans, and daily routines on your own. It is never good for us to oversee our lives. Then add in that we have an enemy who hates God and wants to destroy us.

How did/does sin separate and bring forth death into your own life?

2

THE GOOD NEWS

One thing about God we must all come to understand about is that he is the God of hope. He never leaves us to our problems, or in this case our sin, without providing a way of escape. The message of the cross is one of eternal hope found in God's providence. The good news—or gospel as it is known biblically—is that through the sacrifice of Christ, we can have forgiveness of sin and access to God. Entrance is granted because our sin was placed upon a sinless Savior, who willingly took it to the grave. When sin seems to have removed humanity to the point of no return, Jesus steps in and brings us back to the delight of God's kingdom. Second Corinthians 5:21 puts it this way: "That he who knew no sin, became sin, that in him we might become the righteousness of God." Jesus came to earth, lived a sinless life, was crucified and buried, and then resurrected so you and I could have eternal life. This gift of eternal life has a plethora of advantages, but the most important to us must be that we can approach the throne of grace. Because this is such a crucial factor in our salvation, wouldn't it stand to reason that it would be the most contested part of the redemption experience?

For years, I have met people who go through every possible Christian ordinance but have failed in nurturing their personal relationships with God. It is a sad but very common mistake to focus on liturgy, order, or even study without this personal connection to the King himself. I'm being redundant on purpose to allow our thoughts and focus to center back on the true message of the gospel of Christ. That message is that we have forgiveness of sin in order that we might have a relationship with God. As this study progresses, we will illustrate how to have and maintain a healthy relationship with the Lord.

What are some of the things that might creep in and take priority in our personal relationships with God?

In your own words, how could accessing God's throne be instrumental in your daily routine?

3

REPENTANCE FROM SIN AND FAITH IN GOD

Therefore, let us leave the elementary doctrine of Christ and go on to maturity, not laying again a foundation of repentance from dead works and of faith toward God, and of instruction about washings, the laying on of hands, the resurrection of the dead, and eternal judgment.

—Hebrews 6:1–2 ESV

Our initial encounter with the living God should leave us with a complete and total reformation of our hearts. To enter a relationship with Christ, we must be willing to turn from the way we were doing life and toward the new way of living found within God's rule over us. When referring to this process, I often say it is like using jumper cables to start your car. Our new lives in Christ start in the same fashion. Repentance is turning from the negative; faith in God is turning to the positive source of a new life. Although these can be performed independently of each other, neither is effective unless they work in unison. To have repentance from our sin natures is no good unless you combine it with faith in God. Through the years, I have watched people who have done each of these separately, and it never makes for a stable or long-lasting walk with the Lord. To repent alone may leave us clean, but until we begin to pursue the person of Christ, we are just another good citizen. Likewise, to have faith in God without the repentance of sin will leave you with feelings of condemnation and shame. Because this is an ongoing process if we are to follow God effectively, we must learn to combine repentance with faith in the Lord.

Are you learning to allow the Holy Spirit to expose areas of your life that need repentance? What do you do or are doing to expedite these promptings?

Are you developing a hunger or pursuit of the person of Christ? What are some ways that he reveals himself to you?

4

DEVELOPING THE SPIRIT WALK

Probably the most significant change that comes from beginning a walk with Christ is that the Holy Spirit now lives with us. Jesus gives this promise to all who believe and submit to his Lordship.

> If you love me, you will keep my commandments. And I will ask the Father, and he will give you another Helper, to be with you forever, even the Spirit of truth, whom the world cannot receive, because it neither sees him nor knows him. You know him, for he dwells with you and will be in you. (John 14:15–17 ESV)

The fact that the Spirit of God now lives with us should change how we go about our daily routines. It is easy to get caught up in the motions of life and forget that the Lord has made his residence in our hearts. That is why it is crucial from the beginning to develop habits that allow the Holy Spirit to integrate himself into our lives. In this lesson I focus on three things that the Spirit walk requires. The first of those is to learn to hear the voice of the Holy Spirit. The second is to develop a habit of asking the Holy Spirit. And the third aspect is to testify about God's faithfulness and workings in your life. Combining these three things in your everyday life will serve as a firm foundation as you move toward spiritual maturity. Although I am not advocating a rigid structure or formulas in our relationships with God, I am a strong believer in healthy routines. These routines eventually lead to an awareness that the Lord is always with us. Having the primary response of going to God instead of away from him is an essential characteristic of being a disciple. Let's look at how we implement these in our daily routines.

Hearing the Spirit's voice may be easier than you think. Allow yourself the time to discern the voice of the Lord in your daily routine. As you go through the day, remember to write down the things you believe to have come from the Holy Spirit. Make a habit of spending quiet time with the Lord just to listen and decipher those thoughts. In our next chapter, we talk about the importance of scripture. Weighing those thoughts with scripture is crucial for success in this area. God often speaks to us with scripture if we familiarize ourselves with his Word.

Any relationship takes time, including your relationship with God. Remember to allow for mistakes in hearing the Spirit. God has grace for those inaccuracies. But most people don't allow themselves time for the growth process to be implemented.

Take the time to sit quietly before the Lord and write in this space what you hear. Remember to keep a personal journal in the beginning of this process.

The second aspect of walking with the Spirit is that we learn to ask. Asking the Lord is the easiest way to develop a sustaining dependency on him. In human terms, we often think of dependency as a bad thing. But in spiritual terms, this is perhaps one of the healthiest habits to develop. When asked about prayer, Jesus answered with the line from the Lord's Prayer: "Give us this day our daily bread." To ask God is to acknowledge that our sustenance comes from above, not from here below.

There are numerous things that we can ask of the Lord, but

one thing that is often overlooked, especially by new believers, is for wisdom. The wisdom from above will help us to navigate the world around us. This is part of being *in* the world but not *of* the world when we don't try to figure things out on our own. This is also the beauty of having the Lord make dwelling places in our hearts.

Would you link this attribute of asking directly to humility?

What are some of the things that you ask God for routinely?

On a scale of 1–10, how conscious are you of the Holy Spirit in your daily life?

The last aspect of developing a walk with the Spirit is learning to testify to what the Spirit is doing in your life. There is an importance to vocalizing what is spiritually happening to you and the goodness of our God. This is especially fundamental when you are a new believer, and so much has transformed in and around you. That is how reformations and revivals have been fueled throughout history. When those who are young in the faith begin to share their testimonies and proclaim the works of God, it is powerfully motivating.

It is important to remember that this is not bravado or boasting of oneself. Rather, it is simply broadcasting the good news. Developing the habit of testifying is not only to help those outside but encourages and edifies those who are inside the kingdom as well. Remember that you do not have to be a scholar or trained minister to give a testimony. It is simply what you are witnessing. I always refer to the blind man in John chapter 9 who, when questioned about Jesus, said, "One thing I do know, that though I was blind, now I see." Simple words that speak truth always make an impact. One's testimony usually does more than we can imagine to the heart of someone searching for truth.

> Death and life are in the power of the tongue, and those who love it will eat its fruits. (Proverbs 18:21 ESV)

Are you using your words to draw those around you to a knowledge of Christ?

What are some of the practical ways you can use to cultivate this practice of testifying?

5

OUR BELIEF SYSTEM

As we move to the next set of lessons in our process of becoming a disciple of Christ, we explore how we form our beliefs and what the Bible does to align and mold us into the image of Christ. To do this we look at how the sixty-six books were incorporated into what is now the Old and New Testaments to form the Bible. Plus, you will gain understanding of why scripture is needed for daily life and its lasting effects on your character. Perhaps more than any other routine, tool, or discipline we have as followers of Christ, devotion to the scripture is the most essential. Because it is the actual Word of God, we must approach it as holy and with a sense of reverence. Sometimes our familiarity with something can spoil its effect on our lives.

Before you start this lesson, take some time to ask the Holy Spirit to give you a fresh approach to the scripture.

Each of us has an internal belief system, and we will never act contrary to that system. A person always follows this set of internal beliefs whether they are true or not. Because our actions are always subject to these mindsets, it is crucial to learn how to accurately absorb truth and filter it to our beliefs. We start by looking at how our belief systems are formed. And just a note, sometimes it takes more effort not to believe truth than to just take it for what it is. That is an excellent reason for us to unpack this process. There are three principal methods in which we form a belief system: human reasoning, the church, and the Word of God. Sometimes these can intersect in ways that are detrimental to us, but they can also propel us to a greater understanding of truth when applied correctly.

The first method of forming a belief system is human reasoning. Because we have the knowledge of good and evil passed down with centuries of human rebellion against God, this is the most dangerous place from which to draw our beliefs. From ancient philosophy to modern TED Talks, this is something our carnal minds naturally gravitate toward. I heard someone say, "If it feels good, then it must be right." Using one's senses is the primary way that human reasoning becomes integrated into our minds. Like constructing a house without a tape measure, forming beliefs through reasoning can get ugly.

Write down some cultural viewpoints that are centered in human reasoning and how they perhaps shaped our cultural views of truth?

The second way we shape our belief systems is through the church. While it is closer than reasoning to align with God's truth, this method can also get messy. Actuality, the church—those called-out ones—is designed to be the very image and mouthpiece for God. It is our inheritance from the Lord through the new covenant. To speak for and help shape others into Christ's image is the foremost calling for us as believers. But when the church does not align with what is truth, it can become confusing. One of the best and yet dreadful examples of this took place during the time of the Protestant Reformation. The Roman Catholic Church granted something called indulgences to lessen punishment from sin.

Here is an article describing this practice from the historyextra. com website:

As more indulgences were granted, a complex system evolved whereby the church could calculate exactly how much time off purgatory each one was worth. The more time, the bigger the indulgence. There was no limit to what could be granted thanks to the 'treasury of merit', a spiritual bank where the good works and merits of Jesus Christ, the Virgin Mary, Christ's faithful and the saints are collected and can be drawn upon for the remission of sins.

The problem was money. Instead of people earning indulgences through Christian devotion, it became clear that they could be exchanged for a payment. This might be a donation to a charitable cause or, for the wealthy, to have church buildings erected. The bottom line: if you gave the church money, you would be awarded salvation. Such a purchase even came with a receipt, or letter of indulgence. Eventually, it became possible to secure indulgences for someone already dead.

The sale of indulgences continued until the 16th century, a time of religious reform. The abuses formed the basis of German friar Martin Luther's Ninety-Five Theses in 1517, a catalyst document for the Reformation, in which he argued that salvation should be free to all by faith alone; it should no longer be necessary to serve penance for the remission of sins, let alone pay for it.

That same year Pope Leo X offered indulgences to those who gave money to the rebuilding of St Peter's Basilica in Rome. Yet just 50 years later, in 1567, Pope Pius V abolished the sale of indulgences.

It is easy to get into the weeds with all the false doctrines and practices that have evolved over centuries of church history. But I will leave it here, so we can go on to the final and perhaps the only way to securely establish a belief system: the Bible.

Are there certain things you see practiced in church culture that are not based in God's Word? If so, list a few of them here.

The Bible is the only irrefutable method for establishing a belief system that completely aligns with God. Take some time to absorb that statement. Later in this study, we break down the questions you may have as to how I can make such a statement. But for now, let us continue to look at the centrality of scripture to our belief systems. The Bible is and has been the most widespread book across the globe through the ages of. It is more than just a compilation of books about God. Here's what the apostle Peter has to say:

> And we have the prophetic word more fully confirmed, to which you will do well to pay attention as to a lamp shining in a dark place, until the day dawns and the morning star rises in your hearts, knowing this first, that no prophecy of Scripture comes from someone's own interpretation. For no prophecy was ever produced by the will of man, but men spoke from God as they were carried along by the Holy Spirit. (2 Peter 1:19–21 ESV)

Have you ever stopped to think of how divine intervention has kept the scripture intact for thousands of years?

This leads me to a question I get asked a lot: How did we get the Bible, and how did it end up with these sixty-six books? Also what were the circumstances that approved the Bible to be printed in its present form?

6

HOW THE BIBLE WAS FORMED

In the last chapter, we came to the knowledge of how our beliefs are formed. Based on that lesson, we concluded that having the scripture form our beliefs about God and our worldviews is the healthiest, most fundamental process. In this lesson, we explore how the modern Bible was formed and whether that procedure can be trusted. These are common questions for most new believers, but it is good information for any Christ-follower.

The Bibles most of us have sitting on our desks, nightstands, or kitchen tables are comprised of sixty-six books written by different writers that vary in date, language, and context. The Old Testament had standards all its own that were handed down through Jewish history. But we will glance at what most believers use to influence their ways of thinking and characters, the twenty-seven books that form the New Testament. We got these books through a process called canonization. The word "canon" originally meant a measuring reed but morphed into the term "rule" or "yardstick." This is where I adopted the practice of comparing the scripture to a tape measure for living life. Just like building a house without a tape measurer, building our lives void of God's Word does not make for a pretty sight. Without the absolute of the Bible to guide us, we tend to veer off the road.

How we got the canon or rule of scripture is a history lesson too long to reveal in this set of teachings, but there are plenty of resources to draw from for an extended study. For now, I will stick to the basic story line of the New Testament's origin. Scripture, like anything regarding the Lord, must be accepted by faith and believed to be without error. This is not a study to argue the point, but without us hardening this fact, everything else in the discipleship process is without conclusion. Regarding the New Testament, here are four criteria early church councils used to sort out all the circulating letters and books. This process narrowed the field to what we have today.

- Was it written by an apostle or one of their associates?
- Was it accepted and used universally by the churches?
- Did the subject matter stay on track with known scripture?
- Did it bear qualities that spoke of divine inspiration?

Each of these had bearing on the final decision to incorporate these writings into what we now know as the Holy Bible. Keep in mind that apart from what we can see here as a tremendous effort by human beings, the Holy Spirit was working to move upon these men in supernatural ways to present us with the collective scripture.

I mentioned earlier that it sometimes takes a lot of faith to not believe the truth. For us to look at this book as holy, follow its path from development to present day and still not see God's hand in it would take quite the effort. As we push forward, we investigate how the scripture weaves itself into our minds and forms character within people's hearts.

In what ways will understanding the inerrancy of scripture help you to combat the enemy's plan to derail your relationship with God?

Can you think of a time or times when the Holy Spirit brought to your memory a scripture that became a turning point for you? If so, what was that verse(s)?

7

FATHER FILTERED

> But as for you, continue in what you have learned
> and have firmly believed, knowing from whom
> you learned it and how from childhood you have
> been acquainted with the sacred writings, which
> are able to make you wise for salvation through
> faith in Christ Jesus. All Scripture is breathed out
> by God and profitable for teaching, for reproof, for
> correction, and for training in righteousness, that
> the man of God may be complete, equipped for
> every good work.
>
> —2 Timothy 3:14–17 ESV

Now that hopefully you have come to understand that scripture is vital to us as Christ-followers, we move on to how it becomes part of us. As we will see from this passage, the Word of God has a way of weaving itself into our hearts, producing the image of Christ. Unlike any other book ever written, the Bible, when read in union with the Holy Spirit's supernatural power, can transform a person's heart, mind, and character. For this study, we break down the process of how this happens. To do this, we examine verse 16 of the passage above:

> All Scripture is breathed out by God and profitable
> for teaching, for reproof, for correction, and for
> training in righteousness.

The first thing that happens when we meet the scripture is illumination. This is where the Holy Spirit begins to reveal things pertaining to the persons and personalities of the Godhead. It is helpful to note that the Bible is about God. Yes, there are stories and illustrations regarding man, but it is about him and his person. This illumination sets a benchmark for our mindsets and personalities. In this revealing, we learn any errors we may have in our minds and hearts regarding the Lord. All of us have taken the bait at some point and believed a lie about God or how he views us as his children. The worst thing to do at this stage is to try to hide from the light. These can be the moments that Holy Spirit does some of his best work.

The Lord is not trying to expose you for harm but to heal your soul. I earlier I spoke of God always dispensing hope, and these moments are true to that form. Once he has shown you the error, he provides a path of righteousness for us to walk out. Granted, to have any long-term effect on us, we must decide at each step to submit and follow the Holy Spirit's leading, but he always provides a way to move forward.

That brings me to the last thing that occurs regarding the method or process of scripture: when it infuses itself into our characters. The eventual goal of the Word of God is to transform us into the likeness of Christ. The Bible does that when it becomes a part of us through the power of the Spirit. Once this happens, we are never the same. Nor do we deal with the same fears, insecurities, self-esteem issues, and so on.

Now that the process is clear, do you see how and where you have been stopping along this journey? Give a few examples.

Can accepting that the Bible is about God and his redemption plan, change the way you approach scripture as opposed to it being a self-help book? Briefly explain some differences.

8

EVERYDAY PEOPLE

> But according to his promise we are waiting for new heavens and a new earth in which righteousness dwells. Therefore, beloved, since you are waiting for these, be diligent to be found by him without spot or blemish, and at peace.
>
> —2 Peter 3:13–14 ESV

Although being a Christ-follower does not adhere us to a set of rules or regulations, it requires us to be diligent with the lives we live. To be a Christian is to be a person who contributes to any situation encountered because the Holy Spirit is present throughout those situations. Most of what we see in our modern era are people who believe in Jesus for salvation but fail to make it in the growth process. In other words, they are converts but not necessarily disciples. Just the word "disciple" should evoke the idea of discipline. To move forward in the growth process as a believer requires us to have routines or disciplines incorporated into our daily lives. I am a huge fan of these habits because they give us the means that Christ can use to form himself in us. In what has become a classic book on these life habits, Richard Foster describes how these disciplines put you in a place where the Lord can impart his life to you:

> God has given us the Disciplines of the spiritual life as a means of receiving his grace. The Disciplines

allow us to place ourselves before God so that he can transform us.

The apostle Paul says, "he who sows to his own flesh will from the flesh reap corruption; but he who sows to the Spirit will from the Spirit reap eternal life" (Gal. 6:8). Paul's analogy is instructive. A farmer is helpless to grow grain; all he can do is provide the right conditions for the growing of grain. He cultivates the ground, he plants the seed, he waters the plants, and then the natural forces of the earth take over and up comes the grain. This is the way it is with the Spiritual Disciplines—they are a way of sowing to the Spirit. The Disciplines are God's way of getting us into the ground; they put us where he can work within us and transform us. By themselves the Spiritual Disciplines can do nothing; they can only get us to the place where something can be done. They are God's means of grace. The inner righteousness we seek is not something that is poured on. (Richard J. Foster, *Celebration of Discipline*, Apple Books)

If you search the internet, there are dozens of lists that contain these and other life habits you can use for spiritual growth. But this is a compilation of those daily practices I feel have helped most in my life and the lives I have witnessed firsthand.

The first routine that a person can get into is to learn how to communicate with the Lord in what we know as prayer. In an earlier segment, we covered how to hear from and talk with the Spirit of God. Here, however, we will elaborate on this subject because of its centrality to the Christian experience. Praying is more than asking or talking to God. It is a full-time consciousness and inner awareness of his presence in our lives. To know and experience the Lord always only comes through time spent developing this kind of relationship. To do this we must first realize that the Lord wants this type of closeness with us. The apostle Paul uses the phrase, "pray without ceasing," in his letter to the Thessalonians. Probably the easiest way to develop this habit is in a quiet place. The rush of the world around us often tries to push this practice away, but if we can learn his presence in the stillness, we can then carry it into our public lives.

The second practice we must learn is to study and meditate on scripture. Studying scripture is for analytical and educational purposes, whereas meditation is for enjoying the beauty and rhythm of God's expressions. I have held the practice of reading a psalm each evening before bed. It is soothing to my soul and a lot more relaxing than counting sheep. My morning scripture reading is usually more analytical, and I accompany this practice with commentaries or word studies. On our website, seriouswithgod.org, I keep informative lists on favorite study tools, specific authors, and general resources.

Next is something I probably shouldn't write about this close to Christmas, fasting. Perhaps no other routine or discipline works in more mysterious ways than fasting. Fasting has a way of revealing those things that are clogging the spiritual pipeline within us and moving the mountains outside. Almost every time I fast, the Lord reveals an area of either unbelief, unforgiveness, or a carnal mindset that needs to be resolved before he imparts a measure of his grace. The great thing about fasting is that it can expedite the grace of God into your life like nothing else. I write this as one who does not see repentance as a terrible thing but as a means to keep me humble before my King. Fasting in combination with prayer can also shake loose the heavenlies for spiritual warfare and for hearing the heart of God on certain circumstances. When we fast, we are inadvertently saying to God that "Hearing and obeying you are more important than even sustenance right now."

Until this point, most of the disciplines we have discussed were interior, things going on between us and the Lord. Now I'd like to discuss a couple of life practices that will help your inward person but are managed on the exterior. Both must intentionally become not just a habit but a lifestyle. These are the disciplines of simplicity and solitude.

Simplicity certainly imitates the life that Christ lived during his time on Planet Earth. Jesus had very few possessions and let a thief watch over his finances. It seems that he did not place value on what he had but was heavily invested in his life with the Father, friends, and those he could influence for the sake of the kingdom. A good gauge for this would be how much of our prayer time, energy, and resources we spend on earthly goods. When we live a simple lifestyle, these things may come to us, but they do not become the rudder to navigate our choices. It can be something as simple as enjoying a rental for your vacations and not having to own a home there. As a lover of books, it could be that I go to the library instead of buying them. The Western culture of ownership eventually leads to a path of complexity that burdens our souls. Take time to inventory those things that are making your life complex, and start to shift to a lifestyle of simplicity.

The last discipline that I want to review is the practice of solitude. Writing this on the heels of a pandemic that forced most to stay at home for months is delicate, I know. But the truth is that most of us have crowded lives. It is hard to walk away from electronic friends, in-person friends, family, and coworkers to find moments of solitude throughout the day, but it is necessary. The practice of solitude will help to fortify your relationships, including your God relationship, like nothing else. It is as if solitude helps us to align ourselves and to equip us to be with people. A person who cannot operate in solitude will never contribute to relationships but will constantly have a need to take from those relationships. This often takes the form of control or codependency at its unhealthiest level.

Something I read once might be helpful here. Loneliness is inner emptiness, but solitude is the fulfillment of my soul. We must purpose in our hearts to withdraw from people, devices, and noise to really enjoy those things in a healthy manner.

Immediately he made the disciples get into the boat and go before him to the other side, while he dismissed the crowds. And after he had dismissed the crowds, he went up on the mountain by himself to pray. (Matthew 15:22–23 ESV)

It appears the Lord had times when he needed to retreat and regroup too. As we learn to live with God in our lives, it is important to carve out those times when we can pay attention to that still small voice.

What are some key components to developing habits and routines that allow for personal growth?

If I am honest, is my default reaction to seek counsel from others rather than waiting and listening to the Lord?

What are some of the things that can be implemented in your own life that will produce a lifestyle of simplicity?

9

COVENANT RESPONSIBILITIES

If anyone comes to me and does not hate his own
father and mother and wife and children and
brothers and sisters, yes, and even his own life, he
cannot be my disciple. Whoever does not bear his
own cross and come after me cannot be my disciple.
For which of you, desiring to build a tower, does
not first sit down and count the cost, whether he
has enough to complete it? Otherwise, when he has
laid a foundation and is not able to finish, all who
see it begin to mock him, saying, "This man began
to build and was not able to finish." Or what king,
going out to encounter another king in war, will
not sit down first and deliberate whether he is able
with ten thousand to meet him who comes against
him with twenty thousand? And if not, while the
other is yet a great way off, he sends a delegation
and asks for terms of peace. So therefore, any one
of you who does not renounce all that he has cannot
be my disciple.

—Luke 14:26–33 ESV

As we conclude our first section on what I like to call personal
transformation, we now look at the agreement God made with us
and our parts to play in that relationship. Because it was the Lord
who initiated this commitment, it is sometimes easy to forget that

each of us has a role as well as responsibilities to fulfill. While it is true that most of the weight of this covenant falls to the Lord, he gives us a part in his redemption strategy. One thing that helped me early in my walk is that I recognized the line between what Christ has given me through his cross and what constitutes the daily cross I am to bear. If we do not have a good balance of understanding in that area, it can lead to challenges in our relationship.

Recognizing that my right standing before God is only because of Christ and the cross is a very healthy approach. If we try to face life through our own righteousness it will only leave us steeped in condemnation. I must solidify the belief that it is only the blood of Jesus that allows me to have a relationship with God and not works on my part. As a sidenote, perhaps our modern methods of evangelism lead us to believe that Jesus is begging us to accept him and his love for us. Nothing could be further from the truth. It was the Spirit of God that drew you to him; it was not your decision. Of course, we decide if we will follow Christ, but ultimately, he chose you, you did not choose him.

Although it sounds like theological hairsplitting, this is important if you want to walk the fine line between your part to play and performance mode. Through the years, I have witnessed hundreds of people try to perform for God and attempt to impress him with works only to be left in shambles. God is love, and he does not want you to fail. But if we set out on paths of performance, it will only lead to the destruction of our relationships in the end. On the other hand, we do have responsibilities to fulfill, and we must not become complacent about them.

So let's look at this covenant and what it means for us to be a people who bear God's name. The word "covenant" appears several times in scripture before we hear Jesus saying that he would make a new covenant in his blood. In Genesis, we see that God promises not to destroy the earth with flooding again, so he makes a covenant with creation. Every time we see a rainbow in the sky, we are reminded us of God's faithfulness. God also declared covenants with Abraham and his descendants, the nation of Israel through Moses, and the house of David. And in Jeremiah, he speaks of the new covenant that he will make with each of us:

> Behold, the days are coming, declares the Lord, when I will make a new covenant with the house of Israel and the house of Judah, not like the covenant that I made with their fathers on the day when I took them by the hand to bring them out of the land of Egypt, my covenant that they broke, though I was their husband, declares the Lord. For this is the covenant that I will make with the house of Israel after those days, declares the Lord: I will put my law within them, and I will write it on their hearts. And I will be their God, and they shall be my people. And no longer shall each one teach his neighbor and each his brother, saying, "Know the Lord," for they shall all know me, from the least of them to the greatest, declares the Lord. For I will forgive their iniquity, and I will remember their sin no more.' (Jeremiah 31:31–34 ESV)

A covenant is a bond between two individuals that should eventually lead them to a common place in certain areas of their relationship. The first common area that these two must share is in their identities. When we accept this union with God, we accept the fact that he wants to change us into his likeness. We are, as the old-timers would say, bearing his image. This process of taking on God's identity is not easy, especially since we are surrounded by a world that tells us to celebrate our individualities. While it is true that each of us is unique, God wants to impose certain personality traits on us that will mark us as sons and daughters of the kingdom. When Jesus began his public proclamation in Matthew's gospel that we call the Beatitudes, it signified a revolution in the way we are to live our lives and the character he wants us to embody. Turning the other cheek and living generously are contrary to what our flesh nature is accustomed to. God is faithful in that when we walk with him, there are processes that work through our minds, hearts, and souls that allow for an infusion of his character into us. Sometimes this development seems slow; other times it appears to come suddenly. Whatever the case, continue to allow the Lord to impart these traits so that we might become bearers of his image.

I'm not being overly flippant here, but it is the Spirit of God that gets us to, though, and beyond these processes that are usually in the form of life circumstances. If we can trust him that each circumstance is Father-filtered, we can endure the cross. It is God's responsibility to produce fruit in your life; it is your responsibility to continue the path no matter how hard it may seem. I know. This stuff preaches better than it lives, but the fruit that remains is greater than the moments of suffering to get there.

What circumstances are you going through now that may perhaps become future sustenance for God's redemptive plan and development of your character?

The second thing we can expect to share in this agreement with God is that we have the same resources available. Because of our marriage covenant, my wife can use my name for various reasons to purchase, build, or schedule. Case in point, she plans 99 percent of the medical/dental visits in our home, although according to our insurance company, I am listed as the primary insured. This responsibility falls to her because it is the arrangement we have between us. There are other areas this works in, but hopefully you can understand by this example. Likewise, as God's people, we have the authority to use his name to benefit the kingdom in a variety of ways. Although he is the primary source, the church is his bride and has complete responsibility to conduct kingdom affairs while here on earth. It is you and I that are charged with going through life looking for opportunities to speak the name of Jesus as well as to pray for the lost, sick, and hurting. It is also our mandate, as the body of Christ, to serve the least of these, which will examine further in later chapters. Someone once quoted Wayne Gretzky, the hockey player, as saying, "You miss 100 percent of the shots you don't take." Well, might I say that 100 percent of the people we don't pray for never get healed, saved, or delivered in Jesus's name! It is the responsibility of the church to conduct kingdom business while on the planet, and its business is the redemption of souls. We are never supposed to hide ourselves or to confine the church to a religious service or geographic location. It is up to you and me to take the name and power of Christ to a world that is without hope.

How responsive are you to other people's needs and pain? Do you really believe that Christ is their answer?

Do you think that our society is becoming less empathetic toward one another? Could this be a snare from the enemy? How can we avoid being unempathetic?

The last thing we want to look at regarding common areas of covenant is the fact that we share the same relational allies and adversaries. On one hand, there are those who are allied with us in this walk of life, and we should be grateful for those relationships. As I have traveled the globe in twenty years of itinerant ministry, there is one thing I have learned: The Lord has his people positioned in every place imaginable. The body of Christ expands beyond geographic, denominational, and economic borders that sometimes tend to blind us to this fact. I love what the Lord said to Abraham in the Old Testament: "I'll bless those that bless you, and curse those that curse you." I have witnessed this firsthand on so many levels throughout the years. God has a way of connecting us to the people we need to be connected to, those who will bring the greatest influence for his kingdom's sake. Let us never think that we are alone in the battle; that is our adversary's trick to get us discouraged. Whether we like it or not, God's opponents became our own the moment we accepted Jesus's call to follow him. My book *Understanding the Heavens* is a guide to spiritual warfare and illustrates the nature of this conflict. There are also various articles on our website (seriouswithgod.org). You are welcome to dig into this subject further from that platform if needed.

For today's lesson, we look at what it means to have God's enemies as our own. And better yet, to have God as our Father, the ultimate warrior. Through the years I have met plenty of Christians who wanted the war to cease and to live in relative peace. But that is not the reality of the kingdom of God. When we committed to Jesus as our Lord and Savior, we put proverbial bull's-eyes on our backs. Satan wants to destroy God's handiwork, especially those who have the authority to stop him and put him in his place. We have been given the ability to destroy the works of the enemy, just as Jesus did while here on earth. But far too many times, we do not see the enemy for just that. Most of the time we are still trying to wrestle with flesh-and-bone people instead of combatting the real foe. Just the same, there are people who have made themselves enemies of our God. It was not the Lord but these wicked people who decided to promote evil and perverseness over what God calls good. As a covenant follower of Christ, you will never get along with this type of person, no matter how hard you try. They are determined to spew and spread these evil thoughts of God and his church no matter what. Our role is to let them know that God is still just and will not be mocked. Although we are to love people, we should always warn them of the danger of God's impeding judgment if they do not submit to his authority and plan of redemption. Here's an example of how the Apostles handled this sort of person:

> When they had gone through the whole island as far as Paphos, they came upon a certain magician, a Jewish false prophet named Bar-Jesus. He was with the proconsul, Sergius Paulus, a man of intelligence, who summoned Barnabas and Saul and sought to hear the word of God. But Elymas the magician (for that is the meaning of his name) opposed them, seeking to turn the proconsul away from the faith. But Saul, who was also called Paul, filled with the Holy Spirit, looked intently at him and said, "You son of the devil, you enemy of all righteousness, full of all deceit and villainy, will you not stop making crooked the straight paths of the Lord? And now, behold, the hand of the Lord is upon you, and you will be blind and unable to see the sun for a time." Immediately mist and darkness fell upon him, and he went about seeking people to lead him by the hand. Then the proconsul believed, when he saw what had occurred, for he was astonished at the teaching of the Lord. (Acts 13:6–12)

Recognizing that there is a war and that by the nature of our relationships with Christ, we are engaged in that conflict is only the beginning. I would not want each of you to get paranoid about the enemy and live in a state of restlessness or fearfulness. My point is to make you aware of your responsibilities to the covenant and how we are to conduct ourselves in times of conflict. Before we move on to the next section of this book regarding how we are transformed by community, I thought it essential that you recognize your significance in this area.

How much energy have you spent praying for the Lord to take away conflict in your life when it could be the battle you need to engage in?

How much of your prayer life is proactively initiated by the Holy Spirit rather than reactive to circumstances and people?

Section 2

TRANSFORMATION THROUGH LIFE TOGETHER

10

THE LOCAL CHURCH AND GOD'S INTENT FOR COMMUNITY

Now when Jesus came into the district of Caesarea Philippi, he asked his disciples, "Who do people say that the Son of Man is?" And they said, "Some say John the Baptist, others say Elijah, and others Jeremiah or one of the prophets." He said to them, "But who do you say that I am?" Simon Peter replied, "You are the Christ, the Son of the living God." And Jesus answered him, "Blessed are you, Simon Bar-Jonah! For flesh and blood has not revealed this to you, but my Father who is in heaven. And I tell you, you are Peter, and on this rock, I will build my church, and the gates of hell shall not prevail against it. I will give you the keys of the kingdom of heaven, and whatever you bind on earth shall be bound in heaven, and whatever you loose on earth shall be loosed in heaven." Then he strictly charged the disciples to tell no one that he was the Christ.

—Matthew 16:13–20 ESV

Now we come to the part of our discipleship journey that transforms our lives by weaving us together with those who are on the same path and destination. This is something that as a follower of Christ, is deeply embedded within our souls—the desire for community. Yet most believers I have known who are truly serving the Lord have struggled to find it in the modern-day spheres of religious activity. This is not to say that some do find true community within these circles, but for the most part, we must not look at what we now call church as the biblical model for community.

In this next section, we explore what true Christian community is all about, its importance for transformation, and how we can obtain it in our lives. I believe this could be one of the most fundamental things for us to navigate as people of God, which makes it a fertile field for the enemy to create conflict.

The chapter-opening scripture passage is one of few times we see the Lord speaking of and using the term "church." These are the ones he has called out from the world and conveyed into his kingdom. The Greek word is *ekklesia*, and it simply means a gathering or assembling of citizens into a home or public place usually for religious purposes. For us to understand what it is to gather in the Lord's name and be connected by that name, let's break down what this is by first looking at three objectives: What it means to assemble, the function and outcome of that assembly, and how assembly transforms us into mature believers.

First, what does it mean to assemble in the name of Christ, and what part does the average believer play?

> And let us consider how to stir up one another to love and good works, not neglecting to meet together, as is the habit of some, but encouraging one another, and all the more as you see the Day drawing near. (Hebrews 10:24–25 ESV)

I don't know if I have ever heard a more quoted verse than this one concerning our gathering together. Especially if someone can use this scripture to produce guilt pertaining to church attendance. The truth is a majority of churchgoers show up every Sunday without regard for what it truly means to assemble. For our study, I propose a different view of coming together as a Christian community.

Instead of us gathering in a random sequence and letting a handful participate, how would it look if each of us had a part to play? The picture I always get of Christian assembly is that of a jigsaw puzzle. Suppose someone asked us to assemble a puzzle, and we simply put all the pieces on the table and said, "Here it is!" It is sad to say, but most of our modern church meetings have become just like that. There may be preaching, singing, and praying, but by and large, most attendees are simply spectators to an event.

The opposite of this, and what I feel the Bible intends, occurs when we put each piece of the puzzle in place, and we can allow our relationships with God to influence and affect each of the other participants. Like unique pieces of the puzzle, by God's design, each of us carries a certain set of gifts, experiences, and inner witnessings that can edify those with whom we meet. This is why I spend so much time teaching about personal transformation. It is only through a relationship with Christ that we can get to this place in our gatherings. This may sound like a soapbox, but it could be that in the contemporary era, we have created a form and system that allow people to attend our gatherings without ever knowing the Lord on a personal level. Heaven forbid someone could frequent our meetings without ever being convicted of sin, called to repent, taught how to live victoriously, or be coerced into a deeper relationship with the King. On the other hand, let's look at the biblical model for what a Christian gathering should look like.

> For the body does not consist of one member but of many. If the foot should say, "Because I am not a hand, I do not belong to the body," that would not make it any less a part of the body. And if the ear should say, "Because I am not an eye, I do not belong to the body," that would not make it any less a part of the body. If the whole body were an eye, where would be the sense of hearing? If the whole body were an ear, where would be the sense of smell?

But as it is, God arranged the members in the body, each one of them, as he chose. If all were a single member, where would the body be? As it is, there are many parts, yet one body.

The eye cannot say to the hand, "I have no need of you," nor again the head to the feet, "I have no need of you." On the contrary, the parts of the body that seem to be weaker are indispensable, and on those parts of the body that we think less honorable we bestow the greater honor, and our unpresentable parts are treated with greater modesty, which our more presentable parts do not require. But God has so composed the body, giving greater honor to the part that lacked it, that there may be no division in the body, but that the members may have the same care for one another. If one member suffers, all suffer together; if one member is honored, all rejoice together. Now you are the body of Christ and individually members of it. (1 Corinthians 12:14–27 ESV)

What then, brothers? When you come together, each one has a hymn, a lesson, a revelation, a tongue, or an interpretation. Let all things be done for building up. (1 Corinthians 14:26–32 ESV)

It is apparent from these scriptures that the Lord champions our uniqueness and desires that we share that distinctiveness rather than reduce our meetings to being a spectator sport. This perspective of class participation in a church service could possibly be one foreign to most of us who call ourselves believers. Most people I meet know there is something inside them that desires for this type of community and gathering. Yet, the reality is that very few ever experience it. This type of gathering allows us to edify and provoke each other to live lives of holiness and devotion to our Lord. Now, I realize that in the context and timing of this study, most of us have never had to think about these ideas, much less take part in a collective gathering like the Bible describes. But at some juncture, we must change the form to accommodate the function.

Let us not forget that the Lord described his house as one of prayer, which brings me to the next point of this lesson on the local church: the function and outcome of gathering together as believers in the name of Christ.

> About that time Herod the king laid violent hands on some who belonged to the church. He killed James the brother of John with the sword, and when he saw that it pleased the Jews, he proceeded to arrest Peter also. This was during the days of Unleavened Bread. And when he had seized him, he put him in prison, delivering him over to four squads of soldiers to guard him, intending after the Passover to bring him out to the people. So, Peter was kept in prison, but earnest prayer for him was made to God by the church. (Acts 12:4–5 ESV)

> For I know that through *your prayers* and the help of the Spirit of Jesus Christ this will turn out for my deliverance. (Philippians 1:19 ESV; emphasis added)

There are plenty of verses throughout the New Testament that give us glimpses into what it was like to be part of the early church. These passages illustrate what the outcomes of those gatherings could be. It is our responsibility, as the church, to be aware of what the Holy Spirit is doing in and outside our communities. As we seek heaven and intercede for our neighbors, the Lord will prompt our prayers. The church has the authority to push against any darkness and the enemy schemes that come into our spheres. Remember the scripture earlier in this chapter, when Jesus said that whatever we bind and loose will be that way.

> I will give you the keys of the kingdom of heaven, and whatever you bind on earth shall be bound in heaven, and whatever you loose on earth shall be loosed in heaven." (Matthew 16:19 ESV)

The thing to remember here is that we only have this authority when we pray in Jesus's name. Praying in the name of Jesus is more than just using a tagline; it is when we are operating under his authority or following his decree. As we grow in our faith, these types of prayers naturally flow out of our relationship with the Lord and with others.

There appears to be one more function and outcome that the early church was walking in that we should discuss. That is being a light to those outside the kingdom. Christ always expects our gatherings to be places for unbelievers to be exposed to the supernatural workings of our God.

> But if all prophesy, and an unbeliever or outsider enters, he is convicted by all, he is called to account by all, the secrets of his heart are disclosed, and so, falling on his face, he will worship God and declare that God is really among you. (1 Corinthians 14:24–25 ESV)

Not only should the church be praying for God's justice and to hear his heart, we should be ready to respond when the Lord wants to show himself through us. In our present-day church meetings, I have found that a large portion of God's people are frightened of or have no context for the manifestation of his Spirit. When we come together, intercessory prayer and allowing the Spirit to supernaturally manifest should be our main focus. This practice of hearing and obeying the Lord in a corporate setting is one of the most renovating habits we can obtain as believers in Jesus Christ. It is one thing to hear God one on one, but when we allow others to share with us and us with them in the workings of God, it becomes personally transformative. If I had to answer why this is, I would say it is because we are submitting ourselves one to another and recognizing a fullness of Christ that only comes through the whole body. I used to call this interdependency. I believe this is a by-product of one's maturity in Christ. As we mature in faith, it becomes apparent that others cannot take what we have; nor do we desire their giftings. My wife likes to say that the older we get, the more we become comfortable in our skin. Just like the disciples who fought over who is the greatest, it becomes apparent that Christ is and has always been the greatest!

How would you describe community as it pertains to us as believers?

Write down what how you can personally bring others to the body of Christ.

11

MAINTAINING INTEGRITY
AND PURIFYING MOTIVES

Now that we have a good understanding of what Christian community should be, let's look at how we can live it practically. The first thing we come to when creating relationships that produce this type of community is that we must be authentic. I know there are a hundred translations of this topic, but I want to identify authenticity as, being true to who God made you to be and living this out among others.

To get where we need to be on this subject, I pulled information from several resources, but none were more helpful than a series of teachings written by Michael H. Clarensau titled *Journey to Integrity*. In his teaching, Mr. Clarensau uses the illustration of a tree to describe Christian character and how to maintain our footing when challenges arise. For the sake of clarity, I want to go through this analogy with you. There are three parts of the tree that help to produce the good fruit Christ speaks of in the Gospels. These include the roots, the trunk, and the branches. When each of these parts are healthy, our characters will be authentic. This authentic character is what we define as integrity. It is what the Bible refers to as a tree planted by streams of water in chapter 1 of the Psalms. This journey to integrity is something I believe will help you to build authentic relationships that allow you live out your faith. Let's look at this analogy of the tree to define this process.

The roots help us to gather nutrients from the soil, which is God's Word. The Bible is full of kingdom principles that every believer should continually draw from when making decisions and life choices. When we do not follow God's principles, we run into core issues that can affect our hearts and have dire consequences. For example, we assume that the Lord is okay with a certain type of immorality, but in reading the scripture, it is clear there are parameters established for this sort of thing. It is our responsibility to humble ourselves in God's sight, ask him for forgiveness and to show us the path we should take to change this behavior. Without the Bible, there are no absolutes for us to work from. As I've said before, it is like building a house without a ruler, and that house could eventually become a catastrophe.

The next part of the tree we need to examine is the trunk. The trunk represents our value systems and what we deem as the most critical aspects of our lives. When our value systems are out of order, it becomes almost impossible to have a good balance in our daily routines. By drawing our principles from scripture, it becomes clear what we should value most as believers in Jesus Christ. It is interesting how most believers would agree that one's relationship with the Lord is the most valuable thing we possess, but few people actually spend time each day cultivating that relationship. This value system, if not nurtured properly, can throw life for a loop. To be like a tree that gives its fruit in season, we must put our values in order.

The last components of the tree, and certainly those closest to the fruit, are the branches. The branches represent our desires or motives. I will hang out around this subject for a minute because I feel the branches are where most believers get snagged. This seems to be where the enemy likes to get in a power punch, if you will. When your motives are pure, relationships can be authentic. When these motives go unbridled, we do not walk the straight line of integrity. These motives prompt us to do what we do each day and is the driving force behind our decisions.

To get to the core of these motives or desires, we must discuss our four basic, or primary, needs. Every human being has a set of basic needs that must be fulfilled to maintain a healthy life. They are security, identity, acceptance, and significance. As we define and dissect these, we will also give a view to what they look like when maintained through a healthy relationship with Christ. Unless these needs are processed by your soul as provided by Christ, your life experiences, careers, and relationships will become the sources you will look to for provision. Of course, we all have these things active in our lives, but they must never become the sources to fulfill these four basic needs.

The first of these fundamental needs we want to look at is security. Security is so foundational to the human experience. Whether it is a native bushman living in tents or the attorney with a home in the hills, security remains a primary part of our everyday lives. Remember, these motives are common to every person you meet. Although as humans we want to have our priorities in order, if security is not met by the Lord, we will be trapped by whatever we believe will bring us that well-being. In our modern world, this usually takes the form of how much money one can obtain. Jesus said this about the subject of security:

> No one can serve two masters, for either he will hate the one and love the other, or he will be devoted to the one and despise the other. You cannot serve God and money.
>
> Therefore, I tell you, do not be anxious about your life, what you will eat or what you will drink, nor about your body, what you will put on. Is not life more than food, and the body more than clothing? Look at the birds of the air: they neither sow nor reap nor gather into barns, and yet your heavenly Father feeds them. Are you not of more value than they? (Matthew 6:24–26 ESV)

Many people today operate their daily routines and make their decisions based on a need to feel secure. The problem is that there will always be lack if we do not rely on the Lord for these feelings of security. Trust me, there is a life in Christ that brings us to a place of security no matter the surroundings. This life is a life motivated by a trust that God has my needs factored into the plan. As the old song says, "His eye is on the sparrow, and I know he watches me." We must allow the Lord to produce within us a complete trust in him as a Father, and he is faithful to his word.

The second basic is identity. It is a need to know who I am and what I have been placed here to do. This basic need is crucial to our self-worth, especially when we are young adults. In our early youth, this need for identity comes in the form of those we idolize, such as sports figures and celebrities. But eventually this desire to know who I am pulls from relationships that are more tangible. These can derive from teams, clubs, or careers. Or if you are a Christian, perhaps which church I attend. Although not harmful in themselves, none of these are useful unless we can truly say our only source of identity is in Christ.

> I have been crucified with Christ. It is no longer I who live, but Christ who lives in me. And the life I now live in the flesh I live by faith in the Son of God, who loved me and gave himself for me. (Galatians 2:20 ESV)

The process for this identity shift can be a painful one as this scripture likens it to crucifixion. When we allow human relationships to form our identities, they become our masters. It is this identification desire that allows us to be swayed by things other than the voice of the Lord. Each of us must find our identity in Christ. After all, he understands who you are and the purpose intended for your life.

The third basic need that can motivate us to act contrary to our characters as Christians is acceptance. This desire is so dominate in the lives of middle-schoolers and teenagers. But if not submitted to God, it can carry over well into our adult years. In most young people, it is marked by the clothes they wear, their hairstyles, the music they like, and so on. Acceptance from others often lies deep within and is sometimes not easy to detect. As believers, we must resolve in our hearts to allow acceptance to come only from the Lord and our relationships with him. The longing for acceptance can be a power punch to our motivation if we allow people to control these desires.

> But when the fullness of time had come, God sent forth his Son, born of woman, born under the law, to redeem those who were under the law, so that we might receive adoption as sons. And because you are sons, God has sent the Spirit of his Son into our hearts, crying, "Abba! Father!" So, you are no longer a slave, but a son, and if a son, then an heir through God. (Galatians 4:4–7 ESV)

These verses alone are enough to make us realize what gifts we have been given through Christ. We have been brought into the family of God as sons and daughters of the King. What greater acceptance could there be than knowing that the Lord called us out from this world and to himself.

And finally, the subject of significance. Our need for security wants to trust in someone. Our need for identity wants to be like someone. Our need to be accepted wants to be with someone, and the need for significance is the thing that wants a cause to stand for. Christ offers this kind of worth to each person who has ever followed him. There is no greater cause than the work of reconciliation that God has called us to be a part of.

> For we are his workmanship, created in Christ Jesus
> for good works, which God prepared beforehand,
> that we should walk in them. (Ephesians 2:10 ESV)

Finding significance in the kingdom of God is not as complicated as one might think. All we must do is walk in the good works that Christ has for us each day. Whether you are the world's greatest preacher, a businessperson, or a homemaker, it is all the same to God if we are walking with him in those good works. The key to kingdom significance is finding out what God has prepared that day and execute those works accordingly. This alone can fill our inner tanks of the need for significance. One of the beauties of having the Holy Spirit always with us is that we can ask him to illuminate certain areas or needs that are not being fulfilled by the Lord. He is faithful to give us the path and process that will allow our motives to be purified.

To maintain the course of Christlikeness in our lives, we must be willing to bring each of these parts of our trees under Jesus's authority. Only by submitting these to him will we be free to live unhindered by the world's influence and people's opinions. We can walk true to the life and character that Jesus means for us to have. As we continue in our journeys, it should become clear to us how important it is to live authentically. Only when we are living this way can it produce community that reflects Christ to the world outside.

Do you sometimes feel like the apostle Paul when he said the things he wanted to do he couldn't, and the things he didn't want to do he did? Describe some of those things you struggle with.

Do you think God has a plan to give you a life without lack in these areas? If so, what are some action steps you might take to help you?

12

OBSTACLES AND OFFENSES

Moving on in our exploration of community and what it means for us to be transformed by it, let's look at some of the things that could possibly hinder us from walking in unity with other believers. Although I do not suggest that this is an exhaustive list, these are some things that I believe pose a tremendous block in the road to community. For the sake of clarity, I want to group these into a three-part message. Starting with fear(s), I move to unbelief and then conclude with offenses. We will look at how each proves to be a barrier in the Christian community. Even though these are not from the Lord, we will also see how he uses them to strengthen the bonds between us and allows for transformation.

The first item on our list is fear. Fear, like unforgiveness, is common to the human experience. When we have not allowed God to deal with and purify our hearts' motives fear can paralyze us and keep us from participating in the work of the kingdom. As the apostle Paul said to his spiritual son Timothy,

> I am reminded of your sincere faith, a faith that dwelt first in your grandmother Lois and your mother Eunice and now, I am sure, dwells in you as well. For this reason, I remind you to fan into flame the gift of God, which is in you through the laying on of my hands, for God gave us a spirit not of fear but of power and love and self-control. (2 Timothy 1:5–7 ESV)

Notice in the context of this passage that Paul is encouraging him to stir up and use his gift. But fear is hindering him. The type of fear Timothy was experiencing is an age-old tactic Satan uses to keep us out of the game. The KJV translation of the Bible uses the word "timidity," which is accurate considering that this type of fear intimidates us into submission. When we allow fear to rule in our hearts, the consequences become evident. They include not engaging in the community or participating in the work. As I mentioned before, each of us has a set of gifts and talents to be used for the kingdom of God. When we do not do so, we take away from the body as a whole.

I am going to pause here a moment and look at this from God's point of view. He has redeemed you and set you free, and when you do not participate because of fear, you are really telling him, "My emotional safety is more important than helping someone else." This type of intimidation usually takes root when self-awareness is intertwined with the fear of rejection. Thank the Lord that when we focus on him, there is a process to remove this from our lives and allow us to be bold. Each of us deals with fear on different levels, but to be crippled by it is certainly no place for a child of God. If this is happening, it is a good indicator that we are not letting the spirit of adoption fully come into our hearts and remove the shame associated with our flesh and old sin nature.

Jim Elliot, a missionary to Ecuador martyred for his faith, said it best: "It is no fool that gives what he cannot keep and gain that which he cannot lose." Keep this in mind when you are challenged to back down. Whenever fear tries to intimidate you into submission, dwell on God's faithfulness instead.

In the Old Testament, God commanded Joshua to take stones from the river bottom after the Israelites had crossed when the Lord parted the waters. These stones were set up at a place called Gilgal as a memorial to God's faithfulness. We can have mental monuments in our own lives as well. These are places in our memories that we draw from when fear comes. It is a place that says the Lord has done it before, and he will do it again. Don't let fear cripple you because it never ceases to attack our minds as believers. Train your mind to focus on the Word of God and the incredible things he has done in your life.

The next obstacle is unbelief. Unbelief is one of those things that will creep into our hearts very slowly. It is caused by us not acting in faith but giving in to fear. The Bible's original language renders the word unbelief in two forms. The first form of the word unbelief is a stubborn, obstinate rebellion that refuses to obey God and his commands. This is when unbelief has fully taken root in our hearts and minds. Let's look at a scripture that will help you translate this thought:

> As it is said, "Today, if you hear his voice, do not harden your hearts as in the rebellion."
>
> For who were those who heard and yet rebelled? Was it not all those who left Egypt led by Moses? And with whom was he provoked for forty years? Was it not with those who sinned, whose bodies fell in the wilderness? And to whom did he swear that they would not enter his rest, but to those who were disobedient? *So, we see that they were unable to enter because of unbelief.* (Hebrews 3:15–19 ESV; emphasis added)

We see in this passage the root of the reason the Israelites refused to go enter the Promised Land even though the Lord had proved himself strong to them time and time again along their journey. Every time you and I refuse to hear and obey the Lord, our hearts become calloused to his commands. If not put under subjection and repented of, this type of unbelief will eventually turn our hearts to stone. Never think that God is a respecter of persons. If he allowed those Israelites to wander in the wilderness until they died, our hard-heartedness may produce similar consequences. The key here is to understand that in the kingdom of God, we are always moving forward. Only those who have adopted a carnal lifestyle is allowed to stop growing in the fullness of Christ. This is what the old-timers called backsliding. It is simply the point in your journey where you refuse to step out in faith and believe God for his promises. Nothing has inflicted more damage on the Christian community than carnal believers. These are those Jesus told not to enter but to also keep others from going into that deep place of trust in the Lord. Kind of scary to think that we can fall away from God to this point. Hopefully you will never get to the place of stubbornness that you refuse to repent.

Most of us fall into the second rendering of the word unbelief, which is found in scripture passages such as this one from Mark's gospel:

> And someone from the crowd answered him, "Teacher, I brought my son to you, for he has a spirit that makes him mute. And whenever it seizes him, it throws him down, and he foams and grinds his teeth and becomes rigid. So, I asked your disciples to cast it out, and they were not able." And he answered them, "O faithless generation, how long am I to be with you? How long am I to bear with you? Bring him to me." And they brought the boy to him. And when the spirit saw him, immediately it convulsed the boy, and he fell on the ground and rolled about, foaming at the mouth. And Jesus asked his father, "How long has this been happening to him?" And he said, "From childhood. And it has often cast him into fire and into water, to destroy him. But if you can do anything, have compassion on us and help us." And Jesus said to him, "'If you can'! All things are possible for one who believes." Immediately the

father of the child cried out and said, "*I believe; help my unbelief!*" And when Jesus saw that a crowd came running together, he rebuked the unclean spirit, saying to it, "You mute and deaf spirit, I command you, come out of him and never enter him again." And after crying out and convulsing him terribly, it came out, and the boy was like a corpse, so that most of them said, "He is dead." But Jesus took him by the hand and lifted him up, and he arose. And when he had entered the house, his disciples asked him privately, "Why could we not cast it out?" And he said to them, "This kind cannot be driven out by anything but prayer." (Mark 9:17–29 ESV; emphasis added)

I want to point out that Jesus is not focusing on this demon or the boy as much as he is zeroing in on the unbelief that is crippling the situation. I know that droves of people read this scripture and want to pray and fast to exorcise demons. But that is not what the Lord is telling us will be driven out by our prayer; rather, it is this type of unbelief. Remember that just two chapters earlier, these same disciples had cast out many demons by the authority of Jesus. It wasn't that they didn't know what to do with the demons; they didn't know how to handle the father's unbelief. When the father of the boy says, "I believe; help my unbelief," it is a cry of repentance. Unlike the stubborn obstinate rebellion mentioned earlier, this type of unbelief is simply saying, "I have never done this before and certainly do not have the strength to proceed. But please empower me to do this, Lord." This is the heart cry God can work with when it comes to unbelief.

The truth is that all of us have unbelief to a certain degree or in certain specific areas of life. But the Lord wants us to remain humble before him and to carry an attitude of repentance. If fear has been the instrument that has paralyzed the church from utilizing our gifts, then unbelief is the mechanism that keeps us from trusting God fully for an abundant life. When I see people not living a victorious Christian life, it leads me to the conclusion that sometime, unbelief has crept into their hearts. Don't confuse what I am saying about the abundant life in Christ; that doesn't mean success in the world's eyes. This type of life that can remain focused on the King and kingdom regardless of circumstances or if things are running smoothly. When we get bent out of shape due to circumstances and situations, it is usually only a symptom of our unbelieving hearts. Belief in the Lord will have an overcoming effect on our minds and will lead to us make decisions based on obedience rather that self-protection.

This leads into the next topic and possibly the most widely used obstacle that keeps us from not only engaging in community but being transformed by our relationships with others: offense. As I mentioned earlier, when we form community to walk through life with others, it can be one of the most meaningful and transformational experiences we can have as believers. But if this goes wrong, it can be one of the most destructive and emotionally damaging things you will have to face. This is what the Bible says about the damage caused by offense:

> A brother offended is more unyielding than a strong
> city, and quarreling is like the bars of a castle.
> (Proverbs 18:19 ESV)

As I write this, I am reflecting on how much emotional carnage offense has had in my life as well as in the lives of those around me. If we are transformed by our relationships with Christ and through relationships with others, wouldn't it stand to reason that the enemy of our souls would attempt to inflict as much harm in these areas as possible? The Greek word used in the New Testament for offense is *skandalon*, which is the same as the trigger on a snare or mouse trap. The enemy will always offer you opportunities to be offended at those we don't agree with or perhaps misunderstand. If we are inclined to take the bait, that offense will lodge deep into our hearts and root itself in core places within our psyches.

Most people buy into an offense at some point or another, so don't get upset if this has happened to you. Offenses often come because of miscommunications between us as God's people. One of the best things I've learned in my time of walking with the Lord is that none of us have it all together. Most people are dealing with things behind the scenes that we never get to hear about or see. The combatant for offense is always to have enough grace and forgiveness in our hearts to offer it to those in need. This is sometimes hard to do when there are such personality differences. When we accept someone for who he or she is and the person's position in life, we can then allow for transformation to happen in our hearts. Just as we want to be free to be our true selves, perhaps that person does as well.

The kingdom of God is made of a lot of personality types, and we won't always be attracted to them all. But we do not have to be upset with them either. I have had the privilege to be acquainted with many people and groups within the body of Christ through my years as a minister. If we have the correct viewpoint on relationships, it will allow us to receive something transformative from every person that has God inside. After all, they have a different view of the Lord than I do, and just maybe the Holy Spirit will find a way to reveal something of himself to me because of our interaction.

Can you think of some gifts that you have to offer that perhaps fear has kept you from using?

How can feasting on God's Word strengthen you against unbelief?

Is there perhaps an offense that has come into your heart? If so, how will you deal with it moving forward?

13

REPRODUCTION:
THE EVIDENCE OF LIFE

Perhaps one of the most important aspects of community is the ability to reproduce ourselves and the God-qualities we possess on to others. There is perhaps no greater fuel for a Christ community to have than to add to our numbers. Keep in mind that I am not writing this as a way for us to just add bodies to our gathering but to remind us of one of the most central ingredients to a community: new disciples. The book of Acts is always my go-to writing for a look into how the early church looked when adding new people.

> And they devoted themselves to the apostles' teaching and the fellowship, to the breaking of bread and the prayers. And awe came upon every soul, and many wonders and signs were being done through the apostles. And all who believed were together and had all things in common. And they were selling their possessions and belongings and distributing the proceeds to all, as any had need. And day by day, attending the temple together and breaking bread in their homes, they received their food with glad and generous hearts, praising God and having favor with all the people. And the Lord added to their number day by day those who were being saved. (Acts 2:42–47 ESV)

Each time I read this passage it evokes one thought: These people were having fun and serving God with all they had. Perhaps this is the beginning of our process to become inviting to new people, enjoying ourselves as followers of Christ. I'll get on a kick for a minute if you will allow. Because we have plunged ourselves into a spiritual battle when we gather in Jesus's name, it is sometimes hard to find enjoyment, but it is crucial for our corporate survival. Trust me, I understand the weariness that comes to a group of Christians bombarded by the enemy day after day. But we should have a joy about serving our God. The old proverb, "You can catch more flies with honey than vinegar," proves true when inviting new people to gather with us. After all, most people who are seeking the Lord are looking for authentic community just as we are. No one wants to be a part of something that does not possess joy. After all, this is a fundamental part of being a Christian, counting it all a joy.

Which brings me to the transformation that happens when we can utilize our gifts and experiences to help others, especially new believers. Much like parenting is in the natural realm, so discipleship and mentoring others are in the spiritual realm. Here is what the scripture says about helping those younger than you:

> But as for you, teach what accords with sound doctrine. Older men are to be sober-minded, dignified, self-controlled, sound in faith, in love, and in steadfastness. Older women likewise are to be reverent in behavior, not slanderers or slaves to much wine. They are to teach what is good, and so train the young women to love their husbands and children, to be self-controlled, pure, working at home, kind, and submissive to their own husbands, that the word of God may not be reviled. Likewise, urge the younger men to be self-controlled. Show yourself in all respects to be a model of good works, and in your teaching show integrity, dignity, and

sound speech that cannot be condemned, so that an opponent may be put to shame, having nothing evil to say about us. Bondservants are to be submissive to their own masters in everything; they are to be well-pleasing, not argumentative, not pilfering, but showing all good faith, so that in everything they may adorn the doctrine of God our Savior. (Titus 2:1–10 ESV)

I can attribute a great deal of spiritual growth in my own life because others, mainly new believers, were willing to ask questions that stretched me beyond capacity. It doesn't take a theological degree to be real with what you know about the Lord. There was a time in my life when I thought I needed to have an answer to every question, but now I'm okay to tell someone that I do not know. If you are someone just beginning this process, please share your testimony with others. It is the most powerful thing you possess in this arena. How God intervened in our personal lives and changed our hearts is a tremendous gift that we tend to overlook. I guess that sometimes we do not feel as though our stories are interesting enough. When I was a new believer, some of the people who had the greatest impacts on my life never had a jailhouse, drinking, down-in-the-gutter transformational experience with the Lord. They were simply faithful to hearing the Spirit and responding to his voice sometimes at a relatively young age. Nevertheless, this is a miracle not to be taken lightly because we were all captive of sin, and Jesus set us free.

Just like parenting, helping new people can be challenging for us at times. But the joy that comes from helping build others is equally as rewarding. I'm going to attempt to outline a few things that I feel can help you in the journey as you help new believers.

First, be as authentic as you can possibly be with new believers. I can't stress how important this element is at the ground level of our relationships. Even though we tend to think we are good at covering imperfections, most people notice the blemishes. The truth is that it helps people not to try to obtain perfection themselves. This is the stuff the Pharisees of the New Testament were doing, and it gets complex. I have been around churches and people with this sort of condemning attitude, and it is not appealing to most. A resurgence of authentic Christianity has been emerging for years. That people like Francis Chan, John Mark Comer, and other celebrity types have chosen to leave the performance model and get back to the grassroots reality of discipling others is commendable.

The second thing to remember in this process of helping new believers is to stay resolved on the issues that are core to our faith and not to get hung up on those that are not. My wife defines these as spine-and-rib doctrines. You can live and move without a rib, but your spine is critical to any movement. There are some issues such as the divinity of Christ, atonement, sin, and the indwelling of the Holy Spirit that are not negotiable. This is not a comprehensive list, of course, but you get the idea; these are spine issues. On the other hand, there are things such as baptisms, eschatology, apostolic succession, and order of service that are not spinal issues. These things can be debated but must not cause you or the person being discipled to become distracted from the main goal—growing in relationship with the Lord. Too many times these rib issues become a dividing line between us as believers. They have their significance but should never cause a brother or sister to stumble, or worse, to walk away from the Lord.

And lastly, please remember to dispense a lot of grace when discipling others. One of my preferred things to remember when I get frustrated at my children for losing things or not wiping their feet is that they are only kids, doing exactly what kids are supposed to do. And they will eventually grow out of it. We must be patient when we disciple others into the image of Christ. One pastor I used to serve with called it changing diapers. When you are dealing with babies, even Christian babies, you must change some diapers. After all, we did not overcome all our issues in a day, week, or even a year in some cases. When we allow others the grace to make mistakes, it speaks volumes to their souls about the God we serve. Perhaps no other attribute is as close to God's heart as forgiveness and grace. This is how we can maintain our vitality in serving the Lord and serving others. Blessed are the flexible for they won't get bent out of shape.

How does adding new believers to a community help change the atmosphere?

Have you ever made the connection between discipling and parenting? If so, how does this help your approach to new believers?

Section 3

TRANSFORMATION THROUGH SERVING

14

CALLED TO SERVE

Like never before, our generation must learn to appreciate and embrace the value of serving. It is a mechanism the Lord often uses to transform our hearts and mold our characters. Even Jesus was not exempt from serving but certainly could have claimed the right to opt out. When confronted about the issue of who was the greatest, Jesus struck a fatal blow to the carnal ego.

> A dispute also arose among them, as to which of them was to be regarded as the greatest. And he said to them, "The kings of the Gentiles exercise lordship over them, and those in authority over them are called benefactors. But not so with you. Rather, let the greatest among you become as the youngest, and the leader as one who serves. For who is the greater, one who reclines at table or one who serves? Is it not the one who reclines at table? But I am among you as the one who serves." (Luke 22:24–27 ESV)

In this next series of lessons, we focus on what it means to be transformed into the likeness and character of Christ through the avenue of serving. As we serve others, God imparts his heart of selflessness to us and allows for certain kingdom principles to take root. This is partly what the Lord meant when he told us to give our lives, and he would give us his. Nothing comes nearer the core being of God like serving others above ourselves. After all, the scripture is an outline of how God continually thinks of his creation more than himself, starting in Genesis and the fall of man in the garden of Eden.

> And the Lord God made for Adam and for his wife garments of skins and clothed them.
>
> Then the Lord God said, "Behold, the man has become like one of us in knowing good and evil. Now, lest he reach out his hand and take also of the tree of life and eat, and live forever." (Genesis 3:21–22 ESV)

In his loving-kindness, the Lord not only makes garments for these two rebels, but by not allowing them to eat from the Tree of Life, he protects their souls from living in a state of sin forever. That is the essence of godly love, to prefer others to ourselves. The problem comes because of our flesh. The carnal mind, the data source for our fleshly desires, must be condemned to death. Nothing kills our natural man more effectively than putting others and their needs ahead of our own. The Lord desires that serving becomes more than something we must strain out or set up a mission trip to perform. As Christ-followers, serving should be a substantial part of our natures. Every time we make others a priority to ourselves, it deals a fatal blow to our selfish natures.

There are, however, pitfalls to be aware of when we serve others. Sometimes our services are not appreciated or desired. But this is part of God's overarching plan to help you transform. Let me explain this precarious concept for a minute. As the master builder, the Lord works on our hearts while we are working in the lives of others. When we serve someone who is ungrateful, it often helps us to see what is in us as well as that individual. As a minister, one of my roles is to coordinate and execute citywide outreaches with numerous churches, volunteers, and local entities to help the most vulnerable in their communities. As you can imagine, this concept of serving others gets put to the test every time we conduct one of these outreaches. I prepare our participants by letting them in on a secret: Not everyone we love on today will reciprocate our gestures. Some folks are just plain nasty and hard to love on, but after all, wouldn't that be us if not for God's rich mercy in our own lives?

I have found that when we serve those who cannot and do not offer us anything in return, it proves the motives of our hearts as if a mirror to the soul. This is why the Lord asks us to allow serving to be more than just the act of service; it has to become part of who we are. As you begin to serve others, this concept should grow in our hearts and prevail in our thought lives. This is something that, as a believer, you will fight against while you live in flesh. Of course, it gets easier to serve, but that old nature seems to continually pop up its ugly head to derail our motives. Because we live in a world's system that is constantly telling us to look out for ourselves and that we deserve things, it makes it even that much harder to put others ahead of ourselves.

In the next lesson, we look at the individual parts we can play in service to those around us. But as we close out this lesson, let's look at a passage of scripture that clearly defines how Jesus illustrated this principle. After all, this was his last night to spend some quality time with his disciples before he was to be crucified. He could have selfishly rested, relaxed, or been attended to by others as he was about to die for them—and us. But not Jesus. He was focused on the joy that lay ahead.

> Now before the Feast of the Passover, when Jesus knew that his hour had come to depart out of this world to the Father, having loved his own who were in the world, he loved them to the end. During supper, when the devil had already put it into the heart of Judas Iscariot, Simon's son, to betray him,

Jesus, knowing that the Father had given all things into his hands, and that he had come from God and was going back to God, rose from supper. He laid aside his outer garments, and taking a towel, tied it around his waist. Then he poured water into a basin and began to wash the disciples' feet and to wipe them with the towel that was wrapped around him. He came to Simon Peter, who said to him, "Lord, do you wash my feet?" Jesus answered him, "What I am doing you do not understand now, but afterward you will understand." Peter said to him, "You shall never wash my feet." Jesus answered him, "If I do not wash you, you have no share with me." Simon Peter said to him, "Lord, not my feet only but also my hands and my head!" Jesus said to him, "The one who has bathed does not need to wash, except for his feet, but is completely clean. And you are clean, but not every one of you." For he knew who was to betray him; that was why he said, "Not all of you are clean."

When he had washed their feet and put on his outer garments and resumed his place, he said to them, "Do you understand what I have done to you? You call me Teacher and Lord, and you are right, for so I am. If I then, your Lord and Teacher, have washed your feet, you also ought to wash one another's feet. For I have given you an example, that you also should do just as I have done to you. Truly, truly, I say to you, a servant is not greater than his master, nor is a messenger greater than the one who sent him. If you know these things, blessed are you if you do them. (John 13:1–17 ESV)

As you go through your daily routine, has it been a habit to think about others as a precedence to serving yourself?

In times past, what has been your reaction to those who have not acted graciously to your serving them? What about those closest to you as opposed to a stranger?

15

BECOMING INTENTIONAL WITH OUR SERVING

For I know the plans I have for you, declares the Lord, plans for welfare and not for evil, to give you a future and a hope.

—Jeremiah 29:11 ESV

This verse, in context, was spoken to the nation of Israel regarding their exile. It is helpful for us to keep it before our eyes, especially when it comes to serving. I have seen numerous people in the body of Christ who served without individual purpose or delight for the work itself. I understand this may seem contradictory to the last lesson, when I spoke on serving to become selfless, but I will explain further as we move along. When our work or service to the Lord are random, it becomes a task rather than a pleasure. Of course, there are times when the Lord asks us to serve randomly. But the general thought here is that as we mature, we should utilize our giftings and specialized skill sets to serve the kingdom.

When I first became a Christian, I would do whatever was needed just to have an opportunity to be a part of what God was doing in the local church I attended. There was a season when I helped with the sound system for music service and was the person who changed out the transparencies on the overhead projector. That statement is certainly an indictment of my age. Most people reading this may have to google what an overhead projector is! Nevertheless, my point is that when you start to serve, it is generally random.

This allows you to find that sweet spot of service that comes from maturing in the faith. As you grow, just as I did, you will find your place in the body of Christ.

But there is nothing worse than someone who fills a position within the local church who doesn't want to be in that spot. I remember Sunday school teachers when I was young who, I do not think, even liked kids or teaching. This can be a volatile combination when you think about it in the setting of a volunteer opportunity. The wording we would use today is that those teachers created a "toxic environment" for not just a bunch of juveniles but for the kingdom itself. Through the years I've witnessed plenty of this toxicity in the church, and it is not the correct response to God's call for service. One thing we must remember is that as our lives are untangled from sin, we experience new levels of freedom in Christ. With these freedoms come the opportunities to really find our purposes and individual callings in God's kingdom and the church. The reason I am writing this section is to hopefully make an impact on those who find themselves working for God in ways that are not fulfilling. While it is certainly okay to fill in a position to help overall, the danger in holding those positions is that we keep someone who is called to it from stepping up. Ninety percent of all service in a local church, or the kingdom for that matter, is volunteer. It is not easy for someone else to volunteer for a position that is already filled or does not look as though needs their help. Before you ask, I want to say that if there is no one in the local church to fill a position, shouldn't the real question be, does this even need to take place if God isn't sending a person to that position?

This brings us to the obvious question: How do I know what I am called to do? Before I answer that question, let's make it clear that I am convinced that every believer in Jesus Christ has been commissioned by the Lord to serve. Hopefully that takes the place of the misconception that service in the kingdom is only for professional ministry or in church programs. Now back to that question and how I know what God has purposed for me.

Motivation comes from a unique set of gifts that God has given to us that will always have a natural feel when we are in the right position. Here is a passage from the book of Romans that puts this idea into perspective:

> For as in one body we have many members, and the members do not all have the same function, so we, though many, are one body in Christ, and individually members one of another. Having gifts that differ according to the grace given to us, let us use them: if prophecy, in proportion to our faith; if service, in our serving; the one who teaches, in his teaching; the one who exhorts, in his exhortation; the one who contributes, in generosity; the one who leads, with zeal; the one who does acts of mercy, with cheerfulness. (Romans 12:4–8 ESV)

Here the apostle Paul is using the analogy of a body to describe how we are motivated for kingdom service. Sometimes we want these gifts to be things they are not, and that makes serving hard. As easy as it is for one of your body parts to function, that's how easy it is to serve when motivated by the right gifting. I mentor a young man who is one of the best encouragers I know. He realizes that there is a call from God on his life but has struggled to find his niche. Because a large majority of pulpit ministers are teachers, he is always trying to teach to give people what they are accustomed to. It does not come out well, which makes him feel disappointed. But when he can stand before a group of people and give a word of encouragement, everyone is moved by his gift. Just like in this passage of scripture, we cannot compare ourselves with each other when using our God-given talents. The Bible refers to these motivational gifts as a grace bestowed on us by God. When the Lord gives us grace for something, then it just feels natural and will always motivate us.

Which of these gifts described in Romans 12 motivates me?

Here is another scripture to help us understand where to start when finding out what the Lord has gifted us with and where to serve.

> The revelation of Jesus Christ, which God gave him to show to his servants the things that must soon take place. He made it known by sending his angel to his servant John, who bore witness to the word of God and to the testimony of Jesus Christ, even to all that he saw. (Revelation 1:1–2 ESV)

Notice that John was only testifying about the things he had seen and what his experiences were. God doesn't always pull us so far off those things that he has done for us. When I gave my life to the Lord it was a radical conversion experience instigated by a verse of scripture. I went from being a very profound sinner and living the lifestyle that comes with it to becoming a true man of God. And because I know in my heart that Christ can change someone's trajectory in a moment, I love to teach God's Word. It is something that motivates and fuels my passion to serve. No matter how many times I get to teach, whether writing or speaking, it is something that never becomes exhausting. I cannot explain how this feels except that it must be how a bird feels whenever it gets airborne or a fish to water. There is no greater sense of worth than when you can accomplish the purpose the Lord designed you for. To serve intentionally in the kingdom, we must be stirred in the core of our beings. This is where those rivers of living water Jesus mentioned connect with a passion for helping others.

Another practical word of advice here is don't overthink things. God has a way of getting you from point A to point B if you will relax and enjoy serving where you are. To get hung up on all the nuances of serving can be a killer to your desire to serve others. It can be as easy as just walking with the Lord and being available when the opportunity arises.

> On one occasion, while the crowd was pressing in on him to hear the word of God, he was standing by the lake of Gennesaret, and he saw two boats by the lake, but the fishermen had gone out of them and were washing their nets. Getting into one of the boats, which was Simon's, he asked him to put out a little from the land. And he sat down and taught the people from the boat. And when he had finished speaking, he said to Simon, "Put out into the deep and let down your nets for a catch." And Simon answered, "Master, we toiled all night and took nothing! But at your word I will let down the nets." And when they had done this, they enclosed a large number of fish, and their nets were breaking. They signaled to their partners in the other boat to come and help them. And they came and filled both the boats, so that they began to sink. But when Simon Peter saw it, he fell down at Jesus' knees, saying, "Depart from me, for I am a sinful man, O Lord." For he and all who were with him were astonished at the catch of fish that they had taken, and so also were James and John, sons of Zebedee, who were partners with Simon. And Jesus said to Simon, *"Do not be afraid; from now on you will be catching men."* And when they had brought their boats to land, they left everything and followed him. (Luke 5:1–11 ESV; emphasis added)

Notice from this passage that Jesus did not call these guys to be lawyers. He commissioned them as they were. Don't be surprised if the thing that makes the most sense is the very thing that Jesus asks you to be a part of.

What are some of the gifts that you possess and some of the things that motivate you personally?

Is there some area that you cannot stand to see the enemy victorious, or a people you feel must be helped? Is there something unjust that motivates you to serve in that arena?

16

SERVING THOSE OUTSIDE THE KINGDOM OF GOD

Until now, we have used the concept of serving to speak of the activities geared toward those in the household of faith. But for this lesson, we talk about service to those on the outside who have not committed their lives to Christ or those who have wandered from the kingdom. As twenty-first century believers, we must learn to take a different approach to those outside God's covenant and become very missional in our methodologies. Let me explain further because it is so crucial in navigating the seasons we currently live in.

> Go to this people, and say, "You will indeed hear but never understand, and you will indeed see but never perceive. "For this people's heart has grown dull, and with their ears they can barely hear, and their eyes they have closed; lest they should see with their eyes and hear with their ears and understand with their heart and turn, and I would heal them. 'Therefore, let it be known to you that this salvation of God has been sent to the Gentiles; they will listen." (Acts 28:26–28 ESV)

In 1974, Archbishop Fulton Sheen spoke to a conference audience and announced that we are at the end of Christendom. Not the end of Christianity or the end of the church, but the end of Christendom. What he meant was that the political, economic, and social systems that shaped Western culture had come to an end. Since the 1950s, North American countries, especially the United States, have begun to exchange the blessing that comes from a society shaped by Christian values for one that has no absolutes or regard for God's truth. If this statement, which looking back, was completely true, then perhaps it is time for us, the body of Christ, to rethink our approaches to those on the outside of God's covenant. Perhaps instead of viewing Western culture as something the church is a central part of, the world outside the kingdom of God should be viewed in the same manner the early Jewish church looked at the Gentile world. Our position as the church would have to adapt to the same position as that of a missionary to their mission field. The church's overall mindset regarding the society around us is that we are here to stand in truth and proclaim God's principles to a world without absolutes. Many of those who are reading these statements would agree with their fundamental truth but might ask, "What is the best way to apply this reality?"

First, we must determine that God is constantly drawing people outside the kingdom into a relationship with himself. As part of their reconciliation, he allows you and me to be parts of the process. No matter how dark the world around us may seem, the Lord wants the church to be the salt and light. The earth will never be without a witness to the Lord Jesus and the good news of salvation through the cross. You may be one of a thousand people God employs to reach someone's heart. It could be as simple as a kind word or a prayer, but it could also be when they are at the tipping point of conversion. Remember that as God's people, we are not selling tickets to heaven. We are simply proclaiming truth in love. Sometimes the worst thing is trying to go beyond what the Holy Spirit is doing and force your hand. We must be mindful of the process and trust that this is God's work, and we are along for the ride.

Second, we must not withhold the truth of God's Word from anyone, especially those on the outside. When we do not speak truth for whatever reason, it appears that we are complicit with what the world is teaching. I do not say here that you are to overstep your boundaries and speak when the Spirit is not prompting you. I am saying that when things come up in conversations, you are obligated as a citizen of the kingdom of God to speak the truth to those on the outside regardless of how that truth is received, how politically correct it is, or whatever gain it will cost you personally. Here is a story from the book of Acts that illustrates this idea:

> Now at Lystra there was a man sitting who could not use his feet. He was crippled from birth and had never walked. He listened to Paul speaking. And Paul, looking intently at him and seeing that he had faith to be made well, said in a loud voice, "Stand upright on your feet." And he sprang up and began walking. And when the crowds saw what Paul had done, they lifted up their voices, saying in Lycaonian, "The gods have come down to us in the likeness of men!" Barnabas they called Zeus, and Paul, Hermes, because he was the chief speaker. And the priest of Zeus, whose temple was at the entrance to the city, brought oxen and garlands to the gates and wanted to offer sacrifice with the crowds. But when the apostles Barnabas and Paul heard of it, they tore their garments and rushed out into the crowd, crying out, "Men, why are you doing these things? We also are men, of like nature with you, and we bring you good news, that you should turn from these vain things to a living God, who made the heaven and the earth and the sea and all that is in them. In past generations he allowed all the nations to walk in their own ways. Yet he did not leave himself without witness, for he did good by giving you rains from heaven and fruitful seasons, satisfying your hearts with food and gladness." Even

with these words they scarcely restrained the people from offering sacrifice to them.

Paul Stoned at Lystra

But Jews came from Antioch and Iconium, and having persuaded the crowds, they stoned Paul and dragged him out of the city, supposing that he was dead. But when the disciples gathered about him, he rose up and entered the city, and on the next day he went on with Barnabas to Derbe. When they had preached the gospel to that city and had made many disciples, they returned to Lystra and to Iconium and to Antioch, strengthening the souls of the disciples, encouraging them to continue in the faith, and saying that through many tribulations we must enter the kingdom of God. (Acts 14:8–22 ESV)

Paul and Barnabas could have set themselves up to enjoy the outcome of having people adore and elevate them. Whether we like to hear this or not, thousands of modern-day believers have sold themselves to the world's system for notoriety or pleasure. This is not what God intends for his church to be in respect to the world around us. Jesus was clear that we would be *in* the world but not *of* the world. For me to influence others or introduce them to a new truth of God's Word, I must have no regard for the gratifications this world can offer. We must always keep in mind that not only are we servants of the Most High, we are citizens of his eternal kingdom.

The last thing I want to discuss as it relates to serving those outside the kingdom of God is that we must live what we say to be effective. Compromise is devastating when we are engaged in witnessing for Christ. Just like any missionary would do on a foreign field, we must not compromise what we say we believe. If you would say it in a group of believers, then hold to it when you are in the world. This principle could possibly be the most crippling thing for the body of Christ in the last half-century. Jesus wanted us to have some context for this when he mentioned to his disciples that if they denied him before men, he would deny them before the Father. We must realize how important our lives are as God's people and how much we affect those outside the kingdom.

> You are the salt of the earth, but if salt has lost its taste, how shall its saltiness be restored? It is no longer good for anything except to be thrown out and trampled under people's feet.
>
> "You are the light of the world. A city set on a hill cannot be hidden. Nor do people light a lamp and put it under a basket, but on a stand, and it gives light to all in the house. In the same way, let your light shine before others, so that they may see your good works and give glory to your Father who is in heaven." (Matthew 5:13–16 ESV)

How would you describe your mindset when it comes to the church's position in modern society? Are we part of the culture, or should we be missional in our initiatives?

Would you consider yourself to be a good ambassador for Christ to those who are not believers? What would you change about how you serve others?

Conclusion

Navigating the narrow way is certainly no walk in the park. Our lives are being shaped into the image of Christ, and this is sometimes painful. The road that lies ahead may be filled with the loss of relationships, career goals, and mostly the mindsets that keep us from knowing him. Transitioning into the person God created you to be will require a great deal of time and intentionality on your part. But the freedom that is on the other side of transformation is something that can never be compared with worldly measures. To know true freedom is to know the One who liberates us with his plan of redemption. Before the world was formed and before we were formed, God had a plan to make us his own. Whether you are a first-grader or a seasoned theologian, the Lord is faithful to reveal himself according to our hearts' hunger.

If there is anything I've learned in my twenty-five years of ministry, it is that God's desire is for us to come to him in any circumstance. The greatest gifts we possess are our abilities to access the throne of grace. My prayer for you, the reader, is that there will be a revelation of this belief. When Christ died on the cross, the veil was torn from top to bottom in the temple. This is testimony that we have no barriers between us and the Lord except our own willingness to come into this place with God. His presence will be a constant reminder that we serve a living God, not just a historical figure. With this walk of the Spirit comes the opportunity to live this life in an abundant manner. Not the extravagance of earthly treasures, but in an overflowing and victorious way to approach your time on this planet. This place of spiritual maturity will always lead you to the position of being with and serving others.

I want to conclude with a scripture that has become a bedrock for myself and my family through the years. It is a reminder that greater things lie ahead for us who are redeemed by the blood of the Lamb and his eternal faithfulness. May it serve as an anchor for your journey.

> Then I heard what seemed to be the voice of a great
> multitude, like the roar of many waters and like the
> sound of mighty peals of thunder, crying out,
> "Hallelujah!
> For the Lord our God
> the Almighty reigns.
> Let us rejoice and exult
> and give him the glory,
> for the marriage of the Lamb has come,
> and his Bride has made herself ready;
> it was granted her to clothe herself
> with fine linen, bright and pure"—
> for the fine linen is the righteous deeds of the saints.
> And the angel said to me, "Write this: Blessed are those who are
> invited to the marriage supper of the Lamb." And he said to me,
> "These are the true words of God." (Revelation 19:6–9 ESV)

References

The Holy Bible, English Standard Version. (2001). Crossway.

The Holy Bible, English Standard Version. (2016). Bible Gateway.

<https://www.biblegateway.com/versions/English-Standard-Version-ESV-Bible/> (Original work published 2001)

Wilkes, Jonny (Sept 2, 2021) https://www.historyextra.com/period/medieval/indulgences-catholic-church-what-why-sold-absolution-sin-reformaton

Foster, Richard J. (1978) Celebration of discipline, *the path to spiritual growth 1ˢᵗ ed.* Harper & Row

Clarensau, Michael (January 1, 1997) Journey to integrity: Developing Christian character (Spiritual discovery series) Gospel Publishing House

·

Printed in the United States
by Baker & Taylor Publisher Services